THIS BOOK
BELONGS TO:

I'M 70
AND
LLAMAZING

HELLO
SEVENTY

A LITTLE BIRD TOLD ME
IT'S YOUR BIRTHDAY.
SO I ATE IT.

I AM
69+

I'VE DECIDED
I'M NOT OLD
I'M 65
PLUS SHIPPING
AND HANDLING

CONGRATS! YOU'RE
TOO OLD
TO DATE
LEONARDO DICAPRIO
YEARS OLD

YOUR BIRTHDAY
OUTSHINES
THE OTHER 364 DAYS
HAPPY BDAY!

70TH
BIRTHDAY
NOT FOR THE WEAK

I TURNED
35
TWICE

CONQUER
THE WORLD
ONE CAKE
AT A TIME

YOU STILL
LOOK 21
(FROM A DISTANCE)

SO
HAPPY
I'M 70
TODAY

HERE'S ANOTHER YEAR TO:
LAUGHING TOGETHER
MESSING TOGETHER
AND MAKING IT TOGETHER

AGE ONLY MATTERS
IF YOU'RE A CHEESE

I'M NOT 70
IT'S MY
FIRST
ANNIVERSARY
OF MY
69TH
BIRTHDAY

TAKE A DEEP BREATH
EAT THE WHOLE CAKE
AND ENJOY THE DAY!

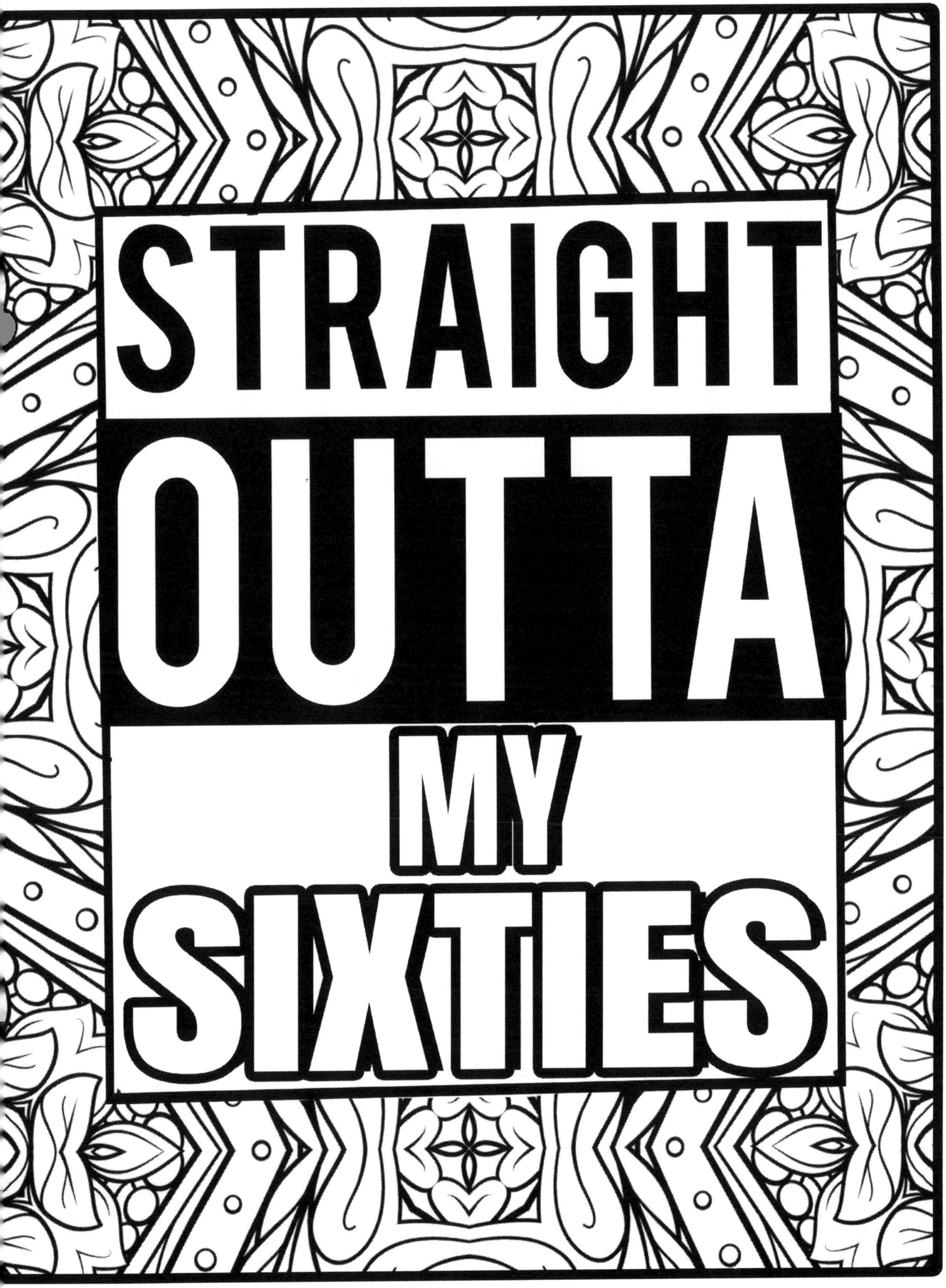
STRAIGHT
OUTTA
MY
SIXTIES

ONE YEAR
CLOSER TO
GRANNY
PANTIES

HUGS, KISSES
AND LOTS OF
BIRTHDAY
WISHES

Made in the USA
Middletown, DE
21 August 2024

59467114R00024